TABLE OF CONTENTS

T0011421

Words in **bold** are in the glossary.

A WALK ON THE WILD SIDE

Want to take a walk on the wild side? Come to the zoo! Seeing different kinds of animals is fun! Zoos don't just need animals. They need people too.

Find out who helps make your visit special. There is a job at the zoo for everyone. Every job is important!

IMPORTANT JOBS

AT ZOOS

by Mari Bolte

PEBBLE
a capstone imprint

Published by Pebble Explore, an imprint of Capstone
1710 Roe Crest Drive, North Mankato, Minnesota 56003
capstonepub.com

Copyright © 2023 by Capstone. All rights reserved. No part of this publication may be reproduced in whole or in part, or stored in a retrieval system, or transmitted in any form or by any means, electronic, mechanical, photocopying, recording, or otherwise, without written permission of the publisher.

Library of Congress Cataloging-in-Publication Data is available on the Library of Congress website

ISBN 9780756572167 (hardcover)
ISBN 9780756572112 (paperback)
ISBN 9780756572129 (ebook PDF)

Summary: Gives readers basic info about often and less often-considered jobs at zoos.

Image Credits
Alamy: Bella Falk, 9, Michiel De Prins, 20, Thomas Wyness, 23, Zuma Press, Inc, 24; Avalon; Handout Pictures, 17; Getty Images: AntonioGuillem, 12, Image Source, Cover (bottom), kali9, 5, Ksenia Semirova/EyeEm, 11, Tanja Luther, 19; Shutterstock: Danny Ye, 27, Jeffrey Isaac Greenberg 9+, 28, Michal Hlavica, 6, Simon_g, Cover (top); The Denver Post via Getty Images: Hyoung Chang/MediaNews Group, 15

Editorial Credits
Editor: Mandy R. Robbins; Designer: Dina Her; Media Researcher: Jo Miller; Production Specialist: Tori Abraham

All internet sites appearing in back matter were available and accurate when this book was sent to press.

Printed and bound in China. PO5132

ZOOOO
WILLKOMMEN

ZOOOO
WILLKOMMEN

ZOO
BERLIN

.zoo-berlin.de

TICKET TAKERS

Before you see any animals, you often see a ticket taker. Everyone needs a ticket to get into the zoo. If you bought a ticket online, a ticket taker checks it. If you still need a ticket, they sell you one.

Do you have a question about the zoo? Just ask them. What time is the animal show? How do you get to the rhino **exhibit**? Where are the bathrooms? A ticket taker can help.

ZOOKEEPERS

Who else works at the zoo? The first person you might think of is the zookeeper. They make sure animals are clean and healthy. They feed and water the animals every day. They clean up pens. They make sure all the gates are closed! Nobody knows the animals at the zoo better than a zookeeper.

Zoo animals need to stay active. They must use their minds and bodies. This is called **enrichment**. Looking for food is a way to get them thinking and moving.

Zookeepers come up with ways to do this. Some animals find their food in logs or holes. Others need to climb high or swim. They may have to solve a puzzle. They could follow their noses. **Predators** might even have to chase down their meal!

FACT

The Moscow Zoo in Russia holds the largest variety of animals. They have more than 24,500 animals and 1,226 different **species**.

VETERINARIANS

Veterinarians, or vets, work closely with zookeepers. They check on every animal at the zoo. If one gets hurt, a vet helps it heal. Baby animals or very old animals might need special attention.

Vets at zoos need to know about a lot of different species. There may be hundreds or thousands of animals at a zoo. Whether it's a tiny fish or a huge elephant, the zoo vet is there to help.

Sometimes, vets from different zoos work together. Some animals are **endangered**. That means they are at risk of dying out. A vet at one zoo may never have seen a certain kind of animal before. But maybe a vet at another zoo has. They can share information. They can learn more about the animals they care for.

> **FACT**
> There are more than 16,300 endangered species around the world.

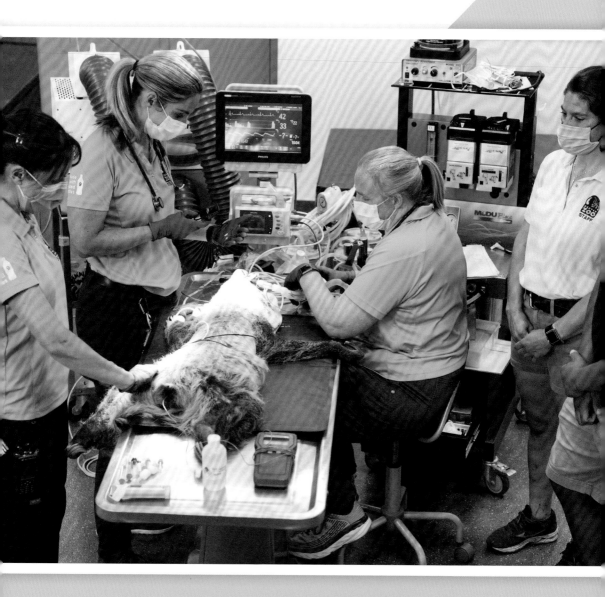

ANIMAL NUTRITIONISTS

Animal **nutritionists** are scientists. They make sure each animal is fed what it needs. Animals need to eat healthy food to feel well. Their needs differ. An elephant eats a lot of fresh fruits and vegetables. But a panther eats meat. And just like people, animals can be picky about what they eat.

FACT

Feeding animals is expensive. The Cincinnati Zoo spends more than $265,000 every year on just fruits and vegetables.

Preparing food for animals is hard work! Take a panda, for example. It can eat 800 pounds of bamboo in a week.

HOUSEKEEPERS

Housekeepers clean up after the people at the zoo. You may not even notice these zoo superheroes. They make sure the floors are not slippery. They pick up trash people leave behind. They clean bathrooms.

Wiping down surfaces keeps them free of **germs**. Washing windows lets the sunshine in and animals see out. The zoo is a clean place to visit thanks to the housekeepers.

CAFÉ WORKERS

Zoos can have big crowds. And big crowds need to eat! Some zoos have food stands. Hot dogs and ice cream are yummy treats!

Large zoos even have cafés. They make food for visitors to sit and eat. They sell quick snacks. They also make hot food for people who want to stay for a meal. Lines move quickly, thanks to café workers. Tables are clean. It is easy to find what you need. Once lunch is over, it's time to see the rest of the zoo!

PERFORMERS

Zoo performers work in live shows. They let people meet the animals up close. Sometimes, a special visitor might even get to touch the animal!

Performers work with zookeepers during live shows. The zookeeper might teach visitors facts about each animal. Knowing an animal's name and where it came from makes visitors want to learn more.

The performer might feed the animal during the show. Some animals, such as seals or birds, might even do tricks. Have your camera ready! You never know what you'll see at a live show.

PROGRAM MANAGERS

Have you ever taken a tour, met an animal up close, or been to a camp at a zoo? Program managers think of ways to bring more people to the zoo. There is always something new to do!

Program managers also think up ways to bring the zoo to people. School visits and news **interviews** are just part of the job. They might even plan your next birthday party!

GIFT SHOP EMPLOYEES

It's almost time to go home. Don't forget the gift shop! Gift shops help raise money to support the zoo's work. Employees there can help you find the perfect way to remember your trip to the zoo. Maybe it's a stuffed animal or a shark's tooth.

Gift shop workers help you find what you need. They make sure the shop's shelves are full of fun things to buy. They help you check out—and make sure you'll want to come back.

Buy
2 less **10%**
Buy
3 or more less **15%**

Buy
3 less **10%**
Buy
3 or more less **15%**

There are many people needed to run a zoo. They are all important. Without one of those people, the zoo would not be a success. Would you like to work at a zoo? What job would you do?

OTHER JOBS AT THE ZOO

Tour guides

Tour guides show people around the zoo. They make sure visitors get to see everything they want to see during their visits. No one gets lost when they're with a tour guide!

Groundskeepers

Groundskeepers keep walking paths, play spaces, and grassy areas clean and neat for visitors. They weed, water, and trim grass, plants, and landscaped areas.

Interns

Interns are students looking for hands-on experience. They assist full-time zoo staff and learn more about what the job requires. Interns can try out many jobs at the zoo.

GLOSSARY

endangered (in-DAYN-juhrd)—at risk of dying out

enrichment (in-RICH-muhnt)—the practice of keeping captive animals active in both the body and mind to keep them healthy

exhibit (ig-ZI-buht)—a display that shows something to the public, such as a captive wild animal

germ (JURM)—a very small living organism that can cause disease

interview (IN-tur-vyoo)—when someone is asked questions to find out about something

nutritionist (noo-TRISH-uh-nist)—a scientist who studies the properties of food and the best foods to eat for a person or animal to be healthy

predator (PREH-duh-tuhr)—an animal that hunts other animals for food

species (SPEE-sheez)—a group of animals that are biologically similar

READ MORE

Davies, Ben Ffrancon. *Behind the Scenes at the Zoo: Your All-Access Guide to the World's Greatest Zoos and Aquariums.* New York: DK, 2021.

Robinson, Syd. *Wild Life!: A Look at Nature's Odd Ducks, Underfrogs, and Other At-Risk Species.* New York: Adams Media, 2021.

Ventura, Marne. *Zookeeper.* North Mankato, MN: Bright Idea Books, an imprint of Capstone Press, 2019.

INTERNET SITES

Bronx Zoo
bronxzoo.com

San Diego Zoo
zoo.sandiegozoo.org/

Smithsonian's National Zoo
nationalzoo.si.edu/

INDEX

ABOUT THE AUTHOR

Mari Bolte is an author and editor of children's books on all sorts of subjects, from graphic novels about science to art projects to hands-on history. She lives in southern Minnesota in the middle of a forest full of animals.